# THE WONDER OF KITTENS

# THE WONDER OF KITTENS

FOG
CITY

PRESS

Published by Fog City Press,
a division of Weldon Owen Inc.
1045 Sansome Street
San Francisco, CA 94111 USA

www.weldonowen.com

weldon**owen**
President & Publisher  Roger Shaw
Associate Publisher  Mariah Bear
SVP, Sales & Marketing  Amy Kaneko
Finance Manager  Philip Paulick
Editor  Bridget Fitzgerald
Creative Director  Kelly Booth
Art Director  Meghan Hildebrand
Senior Production Designer  Rachel Lopez Metzger
Production Director  Chris Hemesath
Associate Production Director  Michelle Duggan
Director of Enterprise Systems  Shawn Macey
Imaging Manager  Don Hill

Library of Congress Control Number on file with the publisher.

ISBN 13: 978-1-68188-096-9
ISBN 10: 1-68188-096-2

10 9 8 7 6 5 4 3 2 1

2016 2017 2018 2019

Printed by 1010 Printing in China.

Have you ever had a kitten
curl up in your lap for a nap?
Or felt the tongue of a kitten
when it licked you? Kittens
are warm little balls of joy
that love to snuggle, romp,
and play wherever they are.

Whether playing hide-and-
seek, climbing up on the roof, or
curling up under your blanket,
these kittens are up to all sorts
of mischievous adventures!

When they are very young, kittens like to stay with their brothers and sisters.

**Fun Fact**

Kittens greet each other by touching their noses together.

## Fun Fact

Newborn kittens first open their eyes when they're five days old.

When they're older, they set out to explore and hunt.

Kittens come in
many colors—
gray, orange,
white, brown—
sometimes all
mixed together.

**Fun Fact**
calico cats have patches of tan, white, and black fur.

## Fun Fact

Kittens' whiskers and ears can tell you their moods.

Kittens love to play peekaboo
and find odd spots to hide.

Fun Fact

A group of kittens
is called a kindle!

So much exploring and playing can tire a kitten out.

Just like us,
kittens use their
noses to sniff
all the smells
around them.

**Fun Fact**

From the day they're born, kittens love to make noise.

And their wide eyes are great
for examining the world.

## Fun Fact

Each front paw has five toes and each back paw has four.

## Fun Fact

Kittens love high places, where they can see everything!

Having places to hide makes kittens feel safe. Kittens can find all sorts of spots to hide—like under a rug, or in small nooks and crannies.

Sometimes you can catch curious kittens climbing walls, rolling around, or even getting a little cheeky—watch out for that pink tongue!

**Fun Fact**
Cats use their tails
for balance-kittens
are still learning!

## Fun Fact

When they grow up, cats have amazing night vision!

Kittens are all born with blue eyes. Their eyes often change color as they grow.

## Fun Fact

Some kittens, called Sphinx cats, have no fur at all!

You can find kittens
with long hair,
short hair, and
medium hair.

And kittens
love to climb
into things—like
boxes, buckets,
or even hats!

## Fun Fact

A kitten's whiskers help detect objects in the dark.

## Fun Fact

Cats need exercise just like humans—they love to be active!

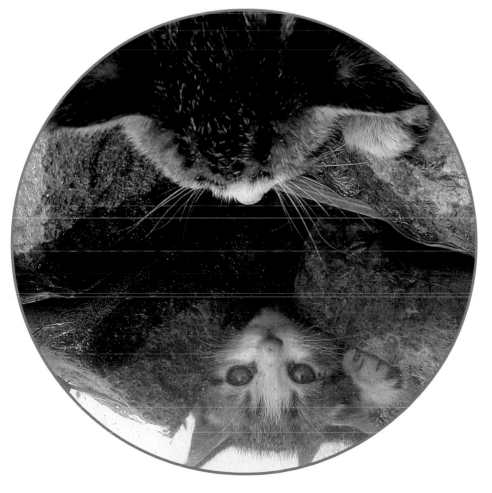

Everywhere
little kittens
go there are
new places
to explore.

Such a big world can be a little
scary for a new kitten . . .

**Fun Fact**

Kittens can sense moods—they know when you're sad.

. . . but they soon adjust—and even learn how to climb trees!

## Fun Fact

Cats love to chew on grass, catnip, and some herbs.

## Fun Fact

Kittens keep warm by forming a big cuddle pile!

A group of kittens born from the same mother at the same time is called a litter.

## Fun Fact

Kittens love to play fight. They know not to be too rough!

Kittens from the same litter often
learn about the world together.

For example,
they might learn
that pianos
can make
a lot of noise—
and so can they!

**Fun Fact**

A kitten meows
mostly at humans,
not other cats.

# Fun Fact

Kittens can sleep for 18 hours a day!

And after a long day of discoveries and frisky romps, there's nothing better than finding a good place to nap.

**Fun Fact**

Kittens can dream, too—they start at about one week old.

Tomorrow will be another
day of new adventures!

Key: SS=Shutterstock; DT=Dreamstime; iSP=iStockPhoto;
LO=Lucky Oliver; t=top, b=bottom

SS: 2, 6, 8, 9, 13, 14, 19, 22, 24b, 25, 27, 28, 31, 32, 34, 35, 37, 39, 40, 41, 42b, 43, 44, 46, 47

iSP: 10, 11t, 20, 21, 29, 30, 33b, 38
LO: 11b, 12t, 17b, 18t, 26, 36b

DT: 4, 12b, 15, 16, 17t, 18b, 23, 24t, 33t, 34, 36t, 42t, 45, 48

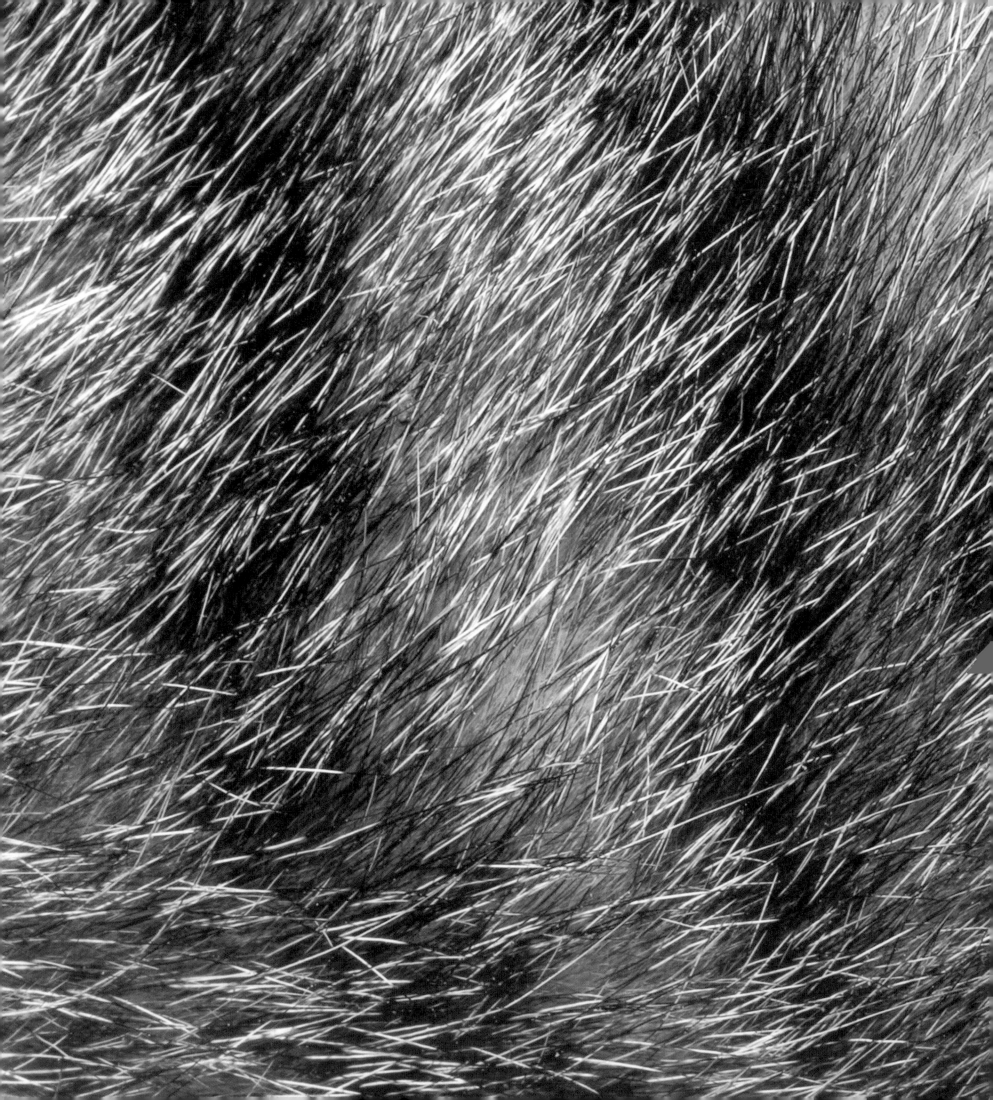